Contents

Meet the planets

A planet is a large, round object. It **orbits** a star. How many planets are there in the **universe**? So many that we can't count them all!

Our solar system is in the universe. The solar system includes a huge star, the sun. It also includes the eight planets that travel around it. Our planet, Earth, is one of these eight planets. Let's learn about Earth and its planet neighbours.

orbit to travel around an object in space

universe everything that exists, including the Earth, the planets, the stars and all of space

Home sweet home

Earth and the other planets get their light from our star, the sun. Planets spin as they orbit. When one side of the Earth turns away from the sun, it is night there. When it turns towards the sun, it becomes day. It takes 24 hours for the Earth to make one full turn.

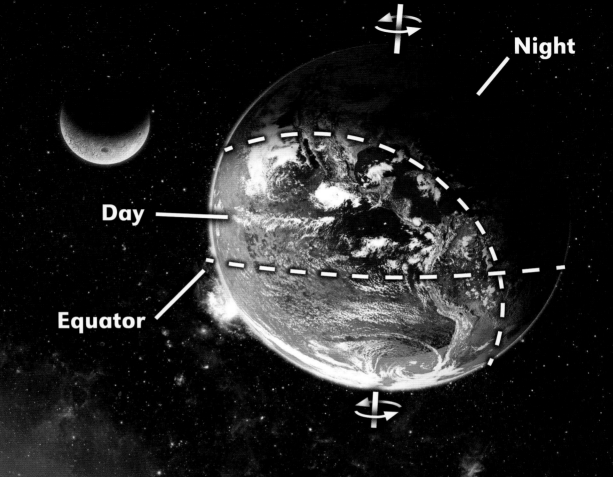

Night

Day

Equator

FAR-OUT FACT

Long ago, planets were called wandering stars.

Take a deep breath. The air is just right for us to breathe. Earth is the perfect planet for life. It is not too cold or too hot. It has plenty of water.

OUR PLACE IN THE UNIVERSE

Raintree is an imprint of Capstone Global Library Limited, a company incorporated in England and Wales having its registered office at 264 Banbury Road, Oxford, OX2 7DY – Registered company number: 6695582

www.raintree.co.uk
myorders@raintree.co.uk

Edited by Hank Musolf
Designed by Kyle Grenz
Media Research by Jo Miller
Production by Kathy McColley
Originated by Capstone Global Library Ltd
Printed and bound in India

978 1 4747 8675 1 (hardback)
978 1 4747 8691 1 (paperback)

British Library Cataloguing in Publication Data
A full catalogue record for this book is available from the British Library.

Acknowledgements
We would like to thank the following for permission to reproduce photographs: NASA, 13 (Both); NASA/ JPL, 12; Newscom: BSIP/JACOPIN, 15, Cover Images/NASA, 19; Shutterstock: Aphelleon, 7, 22, Christos Georghiou, 5, Macrovector, 11, MarcelClemens, Cover (Earth), Robert P Horton, 21, Romolo Tavani, 8, Sunti, 9, Vadim Sadovski, Cover (Planets), 16, 17
Design Elements
Capstone; Shutterstock: Alex Mit, Dimonika, Kanate

Earth is the only planet **scientists** know of that has life on it. But the universe is big. It has so many other planets! Do you think there is life on another planet?

scientist person who studies the world around us

You can look at stars and other planets with a telescope.

Earth's neighbours

Mercury, Venus, Earth and Mars are called the inner planets. They are the closest planets to the sun. These four planets are also called the rocky planets. They formed in a cloud of dust and gas. Heat helped to form them into rocky balls. They are made up mostly of rock and metal.

FAR-OUT FACT

Most of the planets are named after Roman gods.

Mars

Mercury

Earth

Venus

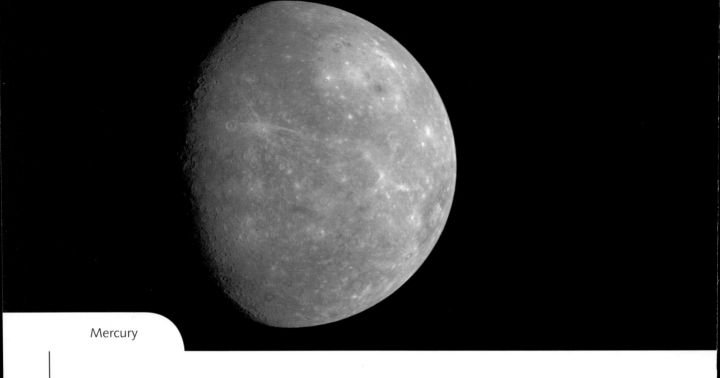

Mercury

Mercury and Venus are the two planets closest to the sun. Mercury is the smallest and fastest planet in the solar system. It speeds around the orbit path. It takes 88 days for it to circle the sun.

Venus is the hottest planet. It is hot enough there to melt metal! Mars is the most like Earth. It has a red tint to it. It is called the red planet.

FAR-OUT FACT

Rovers are unmanned robots with wheels. They have already explored Mars.

Mission to Mars

Soon people should be able to travel to Mars. A company called SpaceX hopes to take people there by 2030. The trip would last about nine months. People would always have to wear space suits there. They wouldn't be able to breathe without them.

The giant planets

Jupiter, Saturn, Uranus and Neptune are the biggest planets in the solar system. The only object bigger than Jupiter is the sun. These four are called the outer planets.

They are furthest from the sun. They are mostly made up of gas. This means a spacecraft could never land on one of them. They are only solid at their core.

Asteroid belt

A belt lies between the inner and outer planets. But it is not the kind of belt you wear around your waist. This belt is the asteroid belt. Asteroids are like smaller planets. Around 2 million asteroids are in the asteroid belt.

asteroid a rocky object in space

asteroid belt

Imagine if all of the asteroids were put together into a ball. They would still be smaller than the Earth's moon.

Uranus

FAR-OUT FACT

The outer planets have more than 140 moons between them. Jupiter has 67. Saturn has more than 60. Uranus has 27. Neptune has 14.

The outer planets are far away from the sun. We could not survive in their freezing temperatures. Uranus and Neptune are nicknamed the ice giants. The outer planets have rings around them made of ice, dust and rocks. Saturn has four groups of rings. They are made of ice.

Planet	Average temperature
Mercury	179°C (354°F)
Venus	482°C (900°F)
Earth	15°C (59°F)
Mars	−63°C (−81°F)
Jupiter	−121°C (−186°F)
Saturn	−125°C (−193°F)
Uranus	−193°C (−315°F)
Neptune	−214°C (−353°F)

Neptune

Planets around other stars

An exoplanet is a planet outside of our solar system. These planets are far away from Earth. No one knows how many of these planets exist. We can't even see them with a **telescope**. We have seen some of them using **satellites**. Satellites are machines that scientists send up into space. They take photographs and collect data for us.

satellite spacecraft that circles Earth; satellites gather and send information to Earth

telescope tool that makes faraway things look closer than they are

FAR-OUT FACT

The closest exoplanet to Earth is very far away. It would take us hundreds of years to get there.

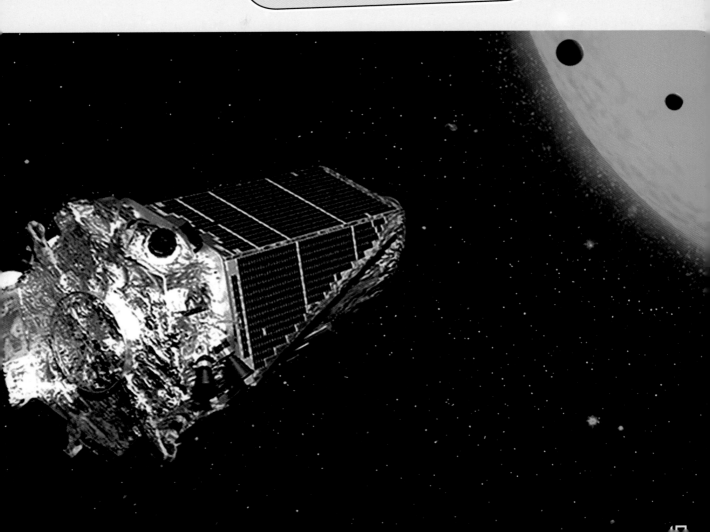

19

Look up!

Don't forget to look up when you are outside at night. You'll see lots of stars and the moon. On some nights, what look like the brightest stars are actually planets! Keep exploring space on your own! What you can learn is truly out of this world!

Venus

Moon

Jupiter

Glossary

asteroid rocky object in space

orbit to travel around an object in space

satellite spacecraft that circles Earth; satellites gather and send information to Earth

scientist person who studies the world around us

telescope tool that makes faraway things look closer than they are

universe everything that exists, including the Earth, the planets, the stars and all of space

Find out more

Big Book of Stars and Planets (Big Books), Emily Bone (Usborne, 2016)

First Space Encyclopedia: A First Reference Book for Children (DK, 2016)

The Inner Planets (Super Space Science), David Hawksett (Raintree, 2019)

Websites

NASA Kids' Club
www.nasa.gov/kidsclub/index.html

National Geographic Kids
www.natgeokids.com/uk/?s=space&post_type=

Comprehension questions

- If you could travel to Mars, would you go? Why or why not?

- Which planet is the hottest?

- How many days would it take for Earth to orbit the sun if it orbited at the same speed as Mercury? How would this make life on Earth different?

Index